How to Hear and Understand the Voice of God.

Dr. Ruth W. Smith

THE VOICE

HOW TO HEAR AND UNDERSTAND THE VOICE OF GOD.

DR. RUTH W. SMITH

© Copyright 2022 – Ruth W. Smith

All rights reserved. No part of this publication may be reproduced, stored in a retrieval system or transmitted in any form or by any means, electronic, mechanical, photocopying, recording or otherwise, without the expressed written permission of the author or publisher.

Scripture references are taken from the King James Version of the Holy Bible unless otherwise noted.

Pronouns for referring to the Father, Son and Holy Spirit are capitalized intentionally, and the words devil and satan is never capitalized.

Publisher: MEWE, LLC
Lithonia, GA
www.mewellc.com

First Edition
ISBN: 978-1-7360565-5-4

For Worldwide Distribution
Printed in the USA

Dedication

To God the Father, God the Son, God the Holy Spirit, my beautiful children, including all my seed, the Body of Christ, Light of the World Christian Tabernacle International, Light of the World Covenant Fellowship International, and all of humanity that God so loved that He gave His Son to die for and His Spirit as a constant companion.

May we purpose to live our lives LISTENING TO FATHER'S VOICE AND OBEYING.

Table of Content

Introduction xi

Recognizing the Voice of God 1

Whose Voice Is It 2

Keys to Recognizing God's Voice 4

Listen and Obey 7

Positioning Ourselves 9

Help from the Holy Spirit 12

Waiting on the Lord 15

Critical Areas to Hear from God 16

How God Speaks to Us 19

About the Author 23

Contact Information 27

Introduction

Of course, we all want to hear the voice of God and know for sure He is the one speaking to us. How do we know it's God and not our imagination, or worse still, the devil putting those thoughts in us? Then again, once we know it's God, how do we understand the message? Before we know His voice, we must understand God's character to know who He is. The Bible says God is love, and generosity is a mark of love. Love is what love does.

When we take the step of fasting and praying, we get a better understanding of how we can hear the voice of God and what it takes to break down those walls and make sure we're not walking in darkness. That is our personal power base.

Now, nobody can fast and pray for you. These are things we have to do for ourselves that strengthen us and give us the power, the anointing, and the connection with God. I love this about being a Christian because God and I are a majority. There is no demon in hell or force that can come against me. Nothing can happen in my life when I am at the center of God's plan and will. Otherwise, I would be just at the mercy of life, people, and circumstances.

However, God has shown us a way to be victorious if we just stay with Him.

I talk to leaders of different nations every day. They all have their own aspirations and issues. But whether we come from the US, Liberia, Nigeria, Ghana, or India, God is the same everywhere. And it's the same devil everywhere too. There is no American, Indian, or Chinese devil; it's the same enemy attacking the body of Christ. And so, when I share my concerns with these leaders, they agree that the biggest problem in their country is people not knowing how to hear from God. Therefore, hearing from God and understanding His voice are critical to us all. If we don't have this connection, we would really miss many opportunities. I can only imagine how different things would be if we really knew how to hear God's voice and understand what He is saying!

- Dr. Ruth W. Smith

Recognizing the Voice of God

Jesus tells us in John 10:1-5:

Verily, verily, I say unto you, He that entereth not by the door into the sheepfold, but climbeth up some other way, the same is a thief and a robber. But he that entereth in by the door is the shepherd of the sheep. To him the porter openeth; and the sheep hear his voice: and he calleth his own sheep by name, and leadeth them out. And when he putteth forth his own sheep, he goeth before them, and the sheep follow him: for they know his voice. And a stranger will they not follow, but will flee from him: for they know not the voice of strangers.

This scripture says we can recognize the true shepherd's voice, Jesus. We know it's Him even when He chooses to speak through the shepherds He has placed over us. Would you say you hear from God? I'm sure you do. And so, don't let the devil tell you that God doesn't talk to you. Because if you are His, He talks to you, and if you are not His, He's still talking because He is trying to draw you to Him. Now, when God talks, the key is to recognize His voice.

You know the shepherd's voice because such a voice sounds like nobody else's. Many can share, teach, and empower, but when you hear the voice of God as a shepherd, it resonates powerfully with your spirit. So, thank God for the shepherd's voice. God uses His vessels to speak to us.

John 10:6 goes on to tell us about Jesus' hearers, ***"This parable spake Jesus unto them: but they understood not what things they were which he spake unto them."*** This also reveals that sometimes, when Jesus is speaking, we may not understand what He is saying. Moreover, we seem to be at a different level of understanding than Jesus because we have not picked up what He is saying in our spirits.

Whose Voice Is It

Now, speaking of understanding the voice of God, we have to make sure we do not assume that all messages we hear within are from God. We think many of the things we listen to are the voice of God, but some of them are not. It is crucial that we know that there is the voice of God, and there is the voice of the devil. Yes—the devil talks to us too. Then there is the voice of our own imagination. Have you ever realized that you have allowed your imagination to lead you on? When you do, you think you're arriving at some kind of truth, only to realize it was just your creative thoughts or emotions talking. This is a big one because I hear a lot of emotional communication, and people think they're hearing from God, whereas it's really their emotions and those of other people doing the talking. We often pick up the emotions of those we trust and think they are telling us the truth. But if they speak out of their emotions, how can we be sure it's true? As for me, I know a few people who, if they say something, I'll believe the opposite. In a way, you need those people around because they help you see a consistent pattern of what the enemy is really up to. So, you coolly say, "Okay, go ahead, tell me some more." Now, you have a clear idea of what the devil is saying to people. And so, you must recognize the people who are talking for who they are and the person talking through them.

There is also the voice of other people and the voice of the environment. Sometimes, in prophetic ministry, we can pick up the vibrations of our environment. We think we are prophesying, but really, we're being influenced by the voices around us. So, we have to ensure that if we are confronting issues, we don't treat them as prophecy. Otherwise, people who are wise and spiritual can see that we're speaking out of environmental pressures, not necessarily the voice of prophecy. We definitely wouldn't want to push our own voice and try to make it prophetic.

And then we have the surroundings. Now, the environment speaks to a more intimate circle, and the surroundings reflect the general space we reside. But we have to be careful not to assume that God is telling us something through these spaces. We want to hear the voice of God, and that alone is what we want to follow. Be aware of distractions so you can shut them down when the environment tries to talk.

Keys to Recognizing God's Voice

First, we must distinguish between hearing God and understanding what He is saying at the moment. When the disciples heard Jesus speaking in parables, they did not understand what He was saying most of the time, so He had to explain the meaning in plain language. For instance, in John chapter 11, Jesus said, ***"Lazarus is not dead; he's asleep."*** But everybody knew Lazarus was dead. They didn't understand what Jesus was trying to say because He used figurative language. The people heard what Jesus was saying, but they didn't know His aim. In other words, we can hear the voice of God and still lack understanding.

And then, when God is speaking to us, we may hear Him and still not even recognize that it is His voice. Samuel the prophet, as a boy, experienced confusion the first time he heard the voice of God (see 1 Samuel 3:8). So, Samuel keeps going back and forth to Eli the priest, asking, ***"Did you call me? What do you want?"*** Finally, Eli tells him, ***"Go back and say, 'Yes, Lord.'"*** Now, Samuel thought it was Eli because sometimes, God will speak to us using voices we trust.

For instance, over the years, I have had visitations from the Late Bishop Jimmie Smith, who co-founded the Light of the World ministry with me. I am confident that it is the Holy Spirit revealing something to me. He comes in that form because Bishop Jimmie is a person I trust. So, God will sometimes visit us in a familiar form, and when He does, we should never think we're having visitations from the world of the dead. Instead, focus on what God is saying.

Also, if we are mentally overwhelmed, we may not even hear God when He's speaking to us. We're so preoccupied that we cannot hear Him with all the clutter in our heads. Much of this can happen in a worship experience where God is talking, but we are too weighed down with our cares to notice Him.

Then we can also be in a setting where we hear an audible voice speaking, but because we're not tuned in, we don't really pick up what the voice is saying. Although we hear a version of what's being said, we don't really capture the essence. We only listen to it superficially, but there's more beneath the surface. And since we can only process one thought at a time, there are gaps in our thoughts.

We are also hearing this static on the line that interferes with the message. When we are in a church setting, we have to be careful not to allow the static on the line to interfere with the message.

That's why journaling is so critical. Journaling keeps us focused. It records what God is saying. It narrows down our thoughts and holds them in check. It keeps us from wandering and getting engaged and delivers us from other mental preoccupations. So, make sure you are present. It's a waste of our time to get in our cars, drive to church, and still not be present.

We will be surprised at how many of us keep attending meetings, but we are all over the place. We say the service was all right. Yes, it was all right because we were not wholeheartedly there. Our body was, but our mind was on the other side of town, as the song says. It's a dangerous thing for our body to be in one place and our mind to be somewhere else.

I thank God I enjoy life because I'm usually present where I am. I give my all wherever I am. If I put enough energy into a situation to get there, then I'm going to give it my fullest attention when I am there.

You **know,** there is a level of disrespect to even be physically present when we don't give the person our fullest attention. When we are with our children, we have to put our cell phone down and get off social media.

I drop my granddaughter at school daily, and I take a lot of calls, especially early in the morning. When the phone rings, I will say, "Can you call me back in about 30 minutes? I'm with my granddaughter right now." I want to make sure I'm present while I'm with her. One day, she said, "Grandma, I just love it when you tell people you're with me, and you will talk to them later." Remember, your total presence is a powerful thing.

Listen and Obey

It's possible to hear God's voice, recognize His voice, understand what He is saying, and then do our own thing. In 1 Samuel 15, when God gave King Saul and his army the order to destroy the enemy totally and not keep anything, guess what? They decided to spare the life of King Agag and keep the choicest animals back because they reasoned they had more value alive. Listen to Saul's excuse:

> *And Saul said unto Samuel, Yea, I have obeyed the voice of the LORD, and have gone the way which the LORD sent me, and have brought Agag the king of Amalek, and have utterly destroyed the Amalekites. But the people took of the spoil, sheep and oxen, the chief of the things which should have been utterly destroyed, to sacrifice unto the LORD thy God in Gilgal.*

Listen, partial obedience is still disobedience. And disobedience is rebellion, and rebellion is witchcraft. Samuel did not mince his words and told it just as if it were the Lord talking.

> *And Samuel said, Hath the LORD as great delight in burnt offerings and sacrifices, as in obeying the voice of the LORD? Behold, to obey is better than sacrifice, and to hearken than the fat of rams. For rebellion is as the sin of witchcraft, and stubbornness is as iniquity and*

***idolatry. Because thou hast rejected the word of the LORD, he hath also rejected thee from being king* (1 Samuel 15:20-23).**

Saul understood it was God talking, and He understood what God was saying. Despite that, he made a conscious decision to disobey God. You know there is no longer any new sacrifice available for willful sin. Anytime we disobey God intentionally, it is rebellion.

God has been too good to us for us to continue in disobedience. If we truly have a heart for God, we will not only take steps to hear his voice, but we will also take the necessary steps to do what He has called us to do.

Positioning Ourselves

Now, the voice of God is very personal, so to hear His voice consistently, we need to have a personal relationship with Him. Often, it is through the Holy Spirit drawing us closer to Jesus. And then we also have to practice listening to Him.

See, you can have a conversation, and things go past your ears, which means you weren't really listening. You didn't give the conversation your undivided attention.

Here's an example of positioning in Exodus 3:2-4 when Moses had his first encounter with the Lord:

And the angel of the LORD ***appeared unto him in a flame of fire out of the midst of a bush: and he looked, and, behold, the bush burned with fire, and the bush was not consumed. And Moses said, I will now turn aside, and see this great sight, why the bush is not burnt.***

And when the LORD ***saw that he turned aside to see, God called unto him out of the midst of the bush, and said, Moses, Moses.***

And he said, Here am I.

Now, a bush burning in the middle of the desert was a common sight. But a bush burning without being consumed by the fire was unusual, and Moses turned to look. This was a sign that he was ready for God to speak to him. He responded immediately, knowing it was the Lord. There needs to be an availability to have that encounter with the Lord and listen out for His voice.

In that posture, the Lord could identify Himself and give Moses his mission statement:

Come now therefore, and I will send thee unto Pharaoh, that thou mayest bring forth my people the children of Israel out of Egypt.

Not only do we have to be willing to obey what He's saying, but we also have to exercise patience when we're communicating with God. He is not on our schedule. So, if we don't know how to exercise patience in dealing with Him, we might go ahead of Him and make a big mess. We have to be patient and wait for the voice of God. Furthermore, we have to position ourselves to hear from God.

Like Habakkuk the prophet, we **will stand upon our watch and wait to see what He will say to us and the answer we shall give** (see Habakkuk 2:1).

Now, one thing about positioning ourselves to hear from God is that we have to make sure we have not already decided what God will say. Our biases and assumptions may neutralize or distort the pure message. Psychologists say when a person speaks, several messages are going out.

1. What is in my mind, which I think I'm saying, because I plan to say them.
2. What is really coming out of my mouth.

3. What the other party hears me saying, which depends on where that person is coming from based on their life experiences.

Ten people may hear the same message, and each of them may be hearing something different because their experiences color what they hear. So, when we're talking to an audience, we have to make sure we are communicating what we want them to hear. I can be saying something entirely different, whereas I thought I was saying the exact message I have in mind.

Go back and record what you speak on tape. You will often find that your mouth was saying things your brain was not saying. This is why we should be prayerful all the more and rely on the Holy Spirit to help us in our weaknesses.

Help from the Holy Spirit

We have to continually pray for messengers of the Word because all kinds of darts are coming from various corners, including things happening in their environment. As a messenger, you have to be sober and alert to disallow interference with what God is saying through you. The more you have people praying for you, the more you can be accurate in bringing forth what God really intended to be said. You can be distracted by how people look when you are delivering a message. The more people look like their minds are wandering or look like their faces are blank, the more distracted you may become, and the less likely you will say all that you intend to say.

Let's look again at how the Lord spoke to young Samuel:

> *And the LORD called Samuel again the third time. And he arose and went to Eli, and said, Here am I; for thou didst call me. And Eli perceived that the LORD had called the child.*
>
> *Therefore Eli said unto Samuel, Go, lie down: and it shall be, if he call thee, that thou shalt say, Speak, LORD; for thy servant heareth. So Samuel went and lay down in his place.*
>
> *And the LORD came, and stood, and called as at other times, Samuel, Samuel. Then Samuel answered, Speak; for thy servant heareth* **(1 Samuel 3:8-10).**

The lesson we learn is that God speaks to us in many ways. We need the Holy Spirit to help us discern His voice. This is how Jesus prayed to the Father before He departed from this earth:

And I will pray the Father, and he shall give you another Comforter, that he may abide with you for ever; Even the Spirit of truth; whom the world cannot receive, because it seeth him not, neither knoweth him: but ye know him; for he dwelleth with you, and shall be in you… But the Comforter, which is the Holy Ghost, whom the Father will send in my name, he shall teach you all things, and bring all things to your remembrance, whatsoever I have said unto you (John 14:16-17, 26).

The Holy Spirit helps us because He is the Spirit of truth. He is the Spirit of revelation, and He shows forth the Father's mind because the Father, Son, and the Holy Spirit are One. We should always ask God to give us the mind of Christ to help us think the way He thinks. It starts by having the Word stored up in us. We can't process what God is saying if we don't have enough of the Word in us.

Again, the Holy Spirit is critical to helping us hear the voice of God. If you have been saved, it is the Holy Spirit who baptizes you into the body of Christ. But there's another level of receiving the Holy Spirit in His fullness, where you allow the Him to fill you up until it overflows. At Babel, God confounded the languages (see Genesis 11). On the other hand, when the Holy Spirit comes, He unifies the languages with God's heavenly language (see Acts 2).

This is why it is so important to have the true Holy Spirit dwelling in us. Now, some people pretend to have the Holy Spirit, but they do not really have Him. You can tell because it sounds like babbling even when they speak in tongues: it brings about confusion. But if you know the Spirit, you can recognize when the Holy Spirit is present.

Waiting on the Lord

So, why do we need to hear from God? So that His will for our lives will be done, and we will not make grievous mistakes. You don't have to do anything except obey God when He gives you a word. If He says, "I'm going to do something," just continue what you were doing until God gives you the signal. He will tell you when to make the shift, and then it all comes together.

I have seen that repeatedly happen in my life. Just know when God speaks to you, you don't really have to start jumping through hoops and trying to help Him out. You can't help Him, anyway. It wasn't your idea; it was His. He will tell you the next step to take. Wait on Him for the next step.

Remember, the Bible says, ***"But they that wait upon the Lord shall renew their strength"*** (Isaiah 40:31). That kind of waiting is not inactivity. That waiting is serving. It is like a waiter or waitress waiting on you by serving you.

So, what do you do when waiting for God to bring the rest of the story to pass? Serve Him. Serve people. Such generosity is an antidote to burnout. Some are burned out because they're preoccupied with themselves rather than finding a way to make somebody else's life better. We are all called to serve the Lord. Jesus declared in John 12:26, ***"…if any man serve me, him will my Father honour."***

Critical Areas to Hear from God

In what areas of your life must you hear from God? There are some major areas where we need to take the time to hear from God. Your **financial stability** is the first one. You have to make good business decisions. Some of you may be in a tight place right now because you took a step of faith in a certain direction. I want to encourage you that it will probably be all right if it was an investment. If it was a consumer item, I have no promises for you. I'm just telling you; we have to get rid of this consumer mentality. Investments will always catch up; eventually, they'll be more valuable than the struggle you're feeling. But when you are obsessed with consumer spending—the car, the television, the latest fashions, and the like—most of those things start to depreciate the moment you take possession of it or drive it out of the parking lot.

Secondly, we need God when it comes down to your **marriage and relationships**. I'm just going to call it your relationships because some of us are single. But in any relationship you're involved in, you need God to guide you. It can't be just about you or your partner if you are married: it has to be God-centered. When you become self-absorbed, then no partner is going to be right. So, we need to seek God about what to do in all important relationships.

Thirdly, we need to hear from God when it comes to **joining and serving in a local church**. We shouldn't be popping up in church whenever it's convenient or hopping from church to church. We need to ask God where we are supposed to be planted. Ask Him who He has selected as your shepherd because He said He would give us shepherds. He never told us to go around town choosing shepherds--this week, I have one pastor and I'm on social media the next week, claiming to have another pastor. No, God is not schizophrenic. He has not given you this pastor and that pastor.

I want to give you a personal testimony. I grew up in Greensboro, Alabama, where I had one pastor. I left and came to Atlanta, where I had a second pastor. I moved from that region to another region, and I had a third pastor. The third pastor was Bishop Jimmie, and he pastored me until he died. Whoever is going to pastor me doesn't have a light job because I'm not going away. God placed me here, and I don't have to be out of here because of some differences. I may have been frustrated in some places, saying things that I regretted, but I had to repent and tell myself to straighten up. Know that God is faithful, and He will bring you back to your center if you listen to His voice. He will fix your finances, your relationships, and how you serve in local churches.

In addition to these things, we need to hear from God concerning our **protection**. I have all kinds of alarm systems and cameras in my home. Yes, I am single, but I'm never alone. We need to pray so that God will dispatch His angels to protect our dwellings. We will never have enough security to keep ourselves; only God can keep us.

The final area where we need to hear from God is in our **dreams and aspirations**. We need to make sure they came from Him, and not us. So, by all means, plan ahead, but make sure you've sought the will of God before you start. ***"Many are the plans in a man's heart, but it is the Lord's purpose that prevails"*** (Proverbs 19:21).

How God Speaks to Us

When God speaks to us, He speaks to us first through the **scriptures**, which inspire, teach, admonish, and correct us (see 2 Timothy 3:16-17). And that's really where you want to get your answers from—the Word of God in context. "In context" means not just randomly picking out a scripture and using it, but making sure the scripture is tied to the situation for which you are using it.

The second way we hear God's voice is by the **Holy Spirit** speaking to our heart. We are God's covenant people, and He has put His laws into our minds and written them in our hearts (see Hebrews 8:10-11).

God speaks prophetically with a **word of knowledge, word of wisdom, or personal prophecy**. 1 Thessalonians 5:20 tells us not to despise prophecy. Prophecy is good. It is for edifying, building you up, and encouraging you. True prophecy points you in the right direction.

In addition, God speaks to us through **God-like counsel**. *"Where no counsel is, the people fall"* (Proverbs 11:14). To be frank, a godly counselor has great wisdom, and to tell you the truth, they are not going to tell you what you want to hear. I will say what the Word of God says in your situation. Remember that there is safety in a multitude of counsel (see Proverbs 11:4).

The next is **confirmation by the mouth of two or three witnesses** (see Matthew 18:16). You can tell your story and get a quick confirmation, and you can ask others, "What do you think God is saying?" This is information. But when God reveals the same thing independently to another, that's confirmation.

So, when we talk about something being established by the mouth of two or three witnesses, these are independent people speaking without your telling them the story. Just because I tell you the story and you agree with me, that is not confirmation. We need to be very clear on this because agreement from people has nothing to do with real confirmation.

Just a few weeks ago, God spoke something in my spirit, and I left and went to Jamaica. And every speaker reiterated what God had spoken to me. They knew nothing about what God had said, and when I got back home, each of the speakers at our church anniversary further confirmed what God had told me, and some things were verbatim, exactly the way God had said it.

So, you don't have to do anything outside the will of God but wait on Him. As you wait, serve until God clarifies what He is saying to you. Colossians 3:15 tells us, ***"And let the peace of God rule in your hearts…"*** A situation may come up, and you pray about it, not knowing what to do, and then, suddenly, peace comes upon you – a peace that surpasses all understanding. In your own natural mind, you think it's crazy, but you feel peace in the situation, and you know it is from God. As I pen this book, I am living in that place right now, just resting in His peace.

And lastly, God speaks through **circumstances**. This is something you don't want to bring upon yourself. You don't want to be disobedient to God and cause Him to allow a circumstance to make you come to your senses. He does this because He loves you. We often tell Him He can have His way with us, and He is saying, "I'm getting ready to do that."

It's better to walk in obedience instead of having Him allow you to go through a humbling or a rerouting process.

I may have been running from a conflict or running from Him until it just blows up. And then I realize I'm dealing with my mistake now. I thank Him when He forgives and redirects me because of His love for me. Just say, "I repent. I couldn't hear You any other way. You have my attention. Thank you, Lord! Amen!" We need to have the courage to confront situations as they arise, and praise God for His faithfulness.

Hearing the voice of God and understanding what He is trying to convey through His messages to you are important for your peace and your successful navigation throughout life's journey. Start with a desire to hear His voice, and then utilize the biblical tools provided throughout this book to help you grow spiritually.

About the Author

Dr. Ruth W. Smith, a native of Greensboro, Alabama, accepted Christ in 1964 and was filled with the Holy Spirit in 1981. She married Pastor Jimmie Lee Smith in 1982. Answering the call to the ministry in 1990, she co-founded Light of the World Christian Tabernacle International and Light of the World Covenant Fellowship International and was later ordained as a minister in 1991.

Under the dynamic leadership of Pastors Jimmie Lee and Ruth W. Smith, The Light grew from 400 to 1,500 members in a 4-year period until Archbishop Jimmie Lee Smith went home to be with the Lord in 2008. The stirring mission of the ministry is to "See a World Without Darkness."

Light of the World Covenant Fellowship International is an organization that mentors and empowers Pastors and Ministries throughout the world. Dr. Ruth was consecrated Archbishop of the organization on July 13, 2008 and became the first woman to serve a worldwide Diocese, overseeing ministries in 26 countries with a membership of over 200,000.

Dr. Ruth's passion for helping people advance the Kingdom of God started from an early age when she participated in the integration of schools in Hale County, Alabama. Through her leadership at The Light, she champions community support through food and clothing drives. In 2013, she received the "Torch Bearer" award by the Southern Christian Leadership Conference (SCLC) in Washington, DC, in recognition of her many years of work as a scholar and spiritual leader committed to the legacy of SCLC founder, Dr. Martin Luther King, Jr.

She recently opened the Jimmie Lee Smith Community Center (JLSCC), which provides Sports, Education and Entertainment to the surrounding communities. Additionally, she established three SateLight locations: LOTW Decatur, December 2015; LOTW South, April 2016; and LOTW Gwinnett, December 2016.

Dr. Ruth holds a Master's degree in Biblical Counseling and a Doctorate in Ministry from Biblical Life College and Seminary in Marshfield, Missouri. She is the published author of three other books, *A Word on Love*, *Keep Moving*, and *Rules of Encouragement*.

She is the proud mother of five children, twelve grandchildren and two great-grandchildren, whom she dearly loves. She is anointed to preach and teach the gospel of Jesus Christ, which she does readily worldwide. Her foundational scripture is Romans 8:28, *"For we know that all things work together for good to them that love God, to them who are the called according to His purpose."*

Contact Information

Ministry
Light of the World Christian Ministries
5883 Highway 155 North
Stockbridge, GA 30281
678.565.7001
thelight@comeintothelight.org
www.comeintothelight.org

Purchasing
678.565.7001
www.comeintothelight.org

Publisher
MEWE, LLC
404.482.3135
mewecorporation@gmail.com
www.mewellc.com

www.ingramcontent.com/pod-product-compliance
Lightning Source LLC
Chambersburg PA
CBHW030046100526
44590CB00011B/347